Jungle Animal Alphabet with Eva and Bobo

Interactive Book for Children

Eva Izogie

Copyright 2022 - All rights reserved.

It is not legal to reproduce, duplicate, or transmit any part of this document in either electronic means or in printed format. Recording of this publication is strictly prohibited, and any storage of this document is not allowed unless with written permission from the publisher except for the use of brief quotations in a book review.

For all the jungle animal lovers.
Enjoy reading, exploring and colouring.

My name is Eva, and I am four years old.
I live in the African jungle with my mum and dad.
I am always happy and never bored because I have many friends in the jungle.

Come with me and meet my friends...

This is Ellie the elephant.

She has large tusks and long a trunk.

This is Zebo the Zebra, all black and white.

And this is Georgie the Giraffe,
he has a long neck and we never lose sight!

And meet my best friend Bobo,
the Vervet monkey, golden and cute.

He lives with his mum and dad in the big tree next to my house.

My mum and dad always give me permission to play with Bobo and my other friends.

We all have fun when we are together.

Today, we are going on a special adventure.

Why don't you join us?

It will be fun!

Write your name here: "*megan*"

Hello "*megan*"

How are you? We are so happy you have joined us.

Look! Ellie, Zebo and Georgie are waiting for you.

Who do you want to ride on?

Ellie?

Zebo?

Or .....

Georgie?

Draw yourself on one of our friends.

Let's go!

We are going to meet all our jungle friends on the alphabet.

Look Bobo!

Look "..Megan..".

Over there! What can we see?

This is an **A**ntelope.

An Antelope has two long horns and eats grass all day.

She has pointy ears. She is beautiful, wouldn't you say?

But wait! What happened to her ears?

Come and take a coloured pencil and colour her ears, have fun!

Read and colour the letter.

This is a Buffalo.

A Buffalo has two big horns and looks like a cow.

He is looking at you "........................" He is so big, wow!

He is walking slowly across the jungle and is asking for your help.

Come and take a coloured pencil and colour her ears, have fun!

Read and colour the letter.

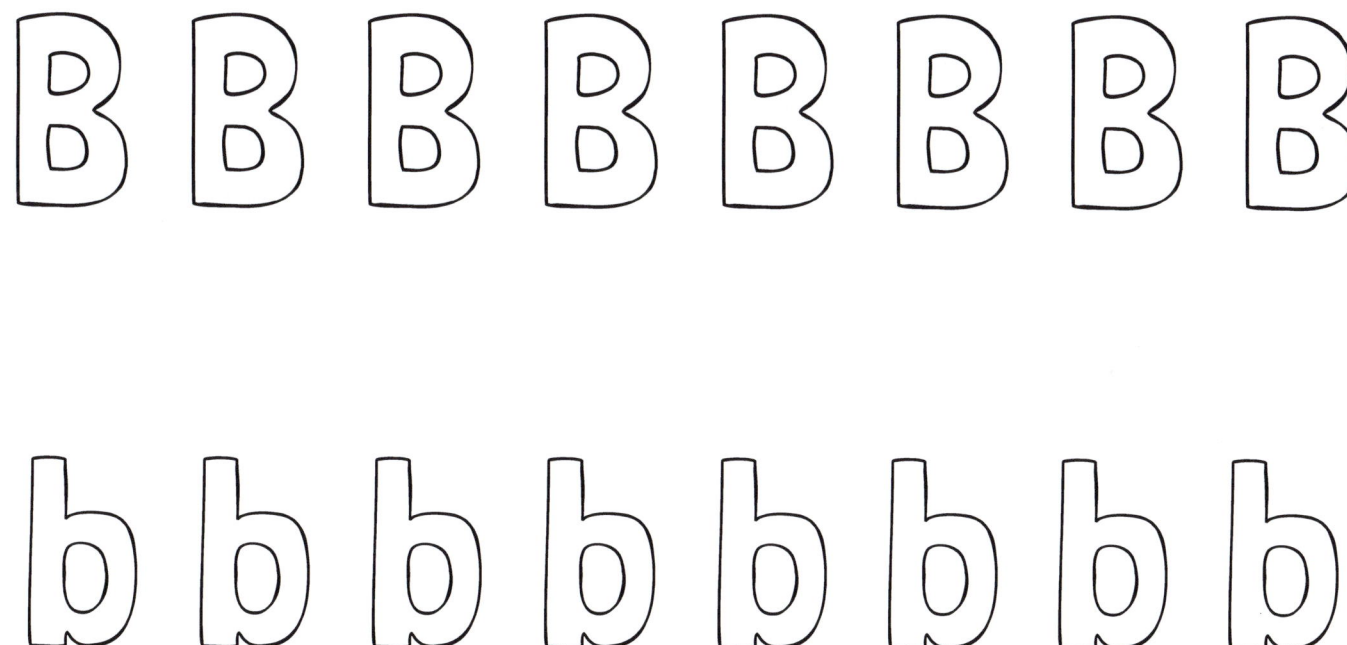

This is a Cheetah.

A Cheetah is a large slim cat, which lives in the jungle.

She has black spots and runs very fast.

By running so fast, she lost some of her spots.

Let's help Cheetah find her spots. Let's do it, there are lots!

Read and colour the letter.

C C C C C C C C

C C C C C C C C

And this is a **D**ragonfly.

A Dragonfly has a long thin body and four large wings.

She loves to fly and looks after the environment.

What happened to the dragonfly's body? It disappeared - it seems!

Let's help the Dragonfly get its colour back.

Read and colour the letter.

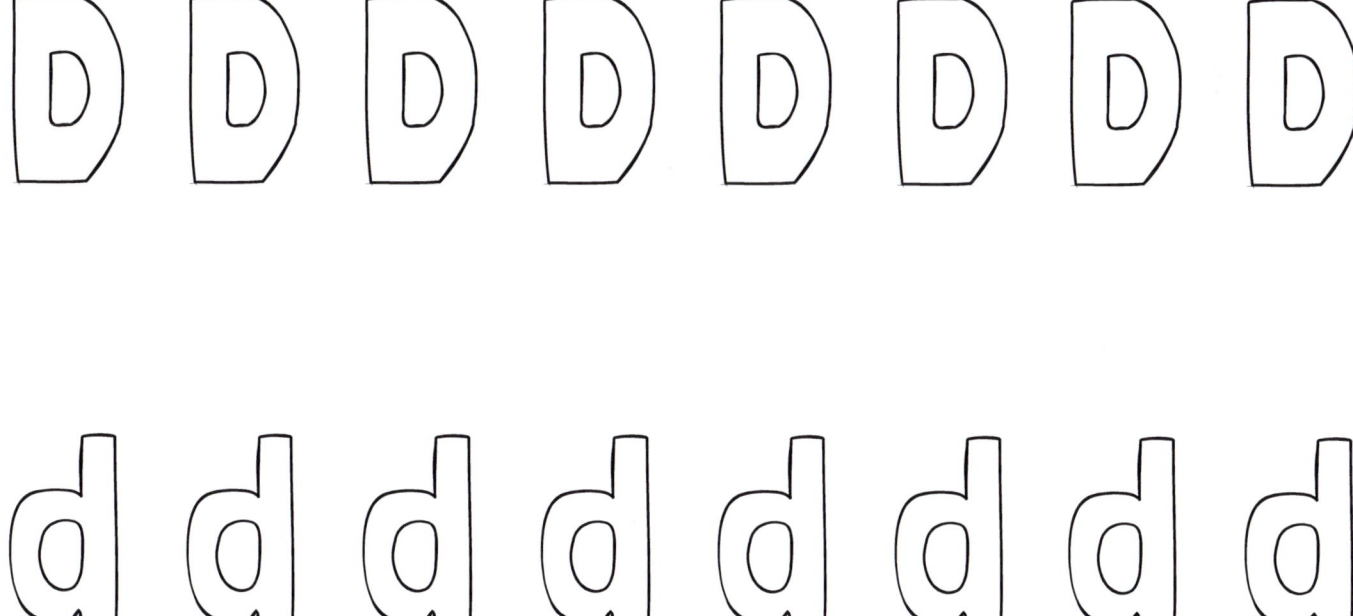

Wow, it's Ellie the Elephant! She is enormous!

Ellie has two big ears, two long tusks and a long trunk.
She is my friend! All big and cuddly.
She is looking at us and asking if you could colour her trunk, please?
It's going to be fun, you'll see.

Read and colour the letter.

E E E E E E E E

e e e e e e e e

Here, we have the **Fox**.

The Fox likes to play all day and he runs very fast too.

He has nice furry hair. Isn't he cute?

He has two big ears to hear other animals from far away.

His ears are usually colour grey! Have fun!

Read and colour the letter.

F F F F F F F F

f f f f f f f f

Look at Georgie, he is a Giraffe.

Georgie has a long neck so he can see very far.

He is tall and has long legs to run fast.

He loves to eat the leaves from very high trees.

Let's colour his neck! Wouldn't that be fun?

Read and colour the letter.

G G G G G G G

g g g g g g g g

And look over there: That is a **H**ippopotamus.

Hippopotamus love to swim in the water.

He is huge but has small ears and eyes.

He stayed in the water the whole day and lost his colour.

Can you colour his body for him to go swimming again, please?

Read and colour the letter.

H H H H H H H H

h h h h h h h h

And what do we have here? This is called an Impala!

An Impala has long thin twisty horns and a short tail.

She can run fast and jump very high.

She is very quiet and likes to eat grass.

Impala is waiting for you to colour her twisty horns.

Read and colour the letter.

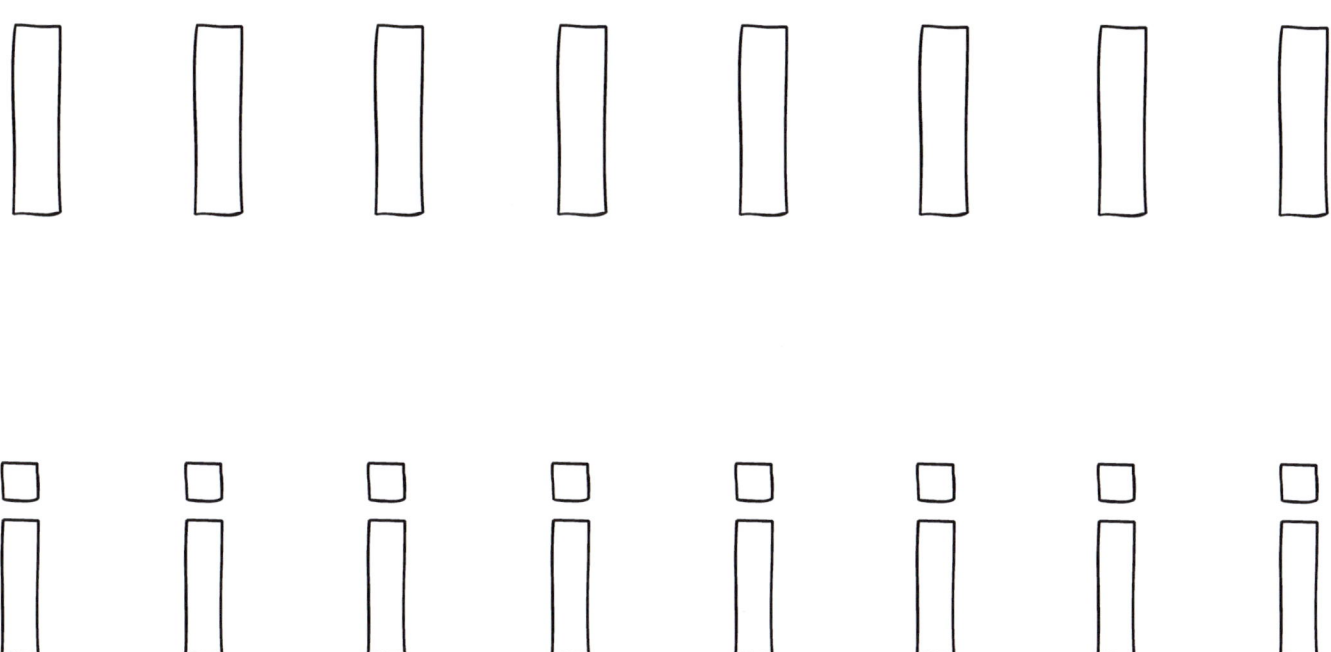

This is a Jackal!

The Jackal loves to hide in tall grass and bushy trees.
She likes to run around and chase other animals near the water.
Her long thin tail has lost its colour whilst running around.
Let's find her tail, It's usually black with a white tip.

Read and colour the letter.

J J J J J J J J

j j j j j j j j

This is a Kudu.

The Kudu is a very shy animal and is similar to an Antelope.
He has two twisty horns and three white stripes on his body.
He likes to just walk around in the jungle whilst eating grass.
Can you please colour his stripes now? It's easy, you know how!

Read and colour the letter.

K K K K K K K

k k k k k k k

Look! This is a Lion.

The Lion is known as the king of the jungle.

He is strong and has golden hair around his head.

Sometimes he just lays and hides in the grass.

Let's colour his hair. Make it nice and furry.

Read and colour the letter.

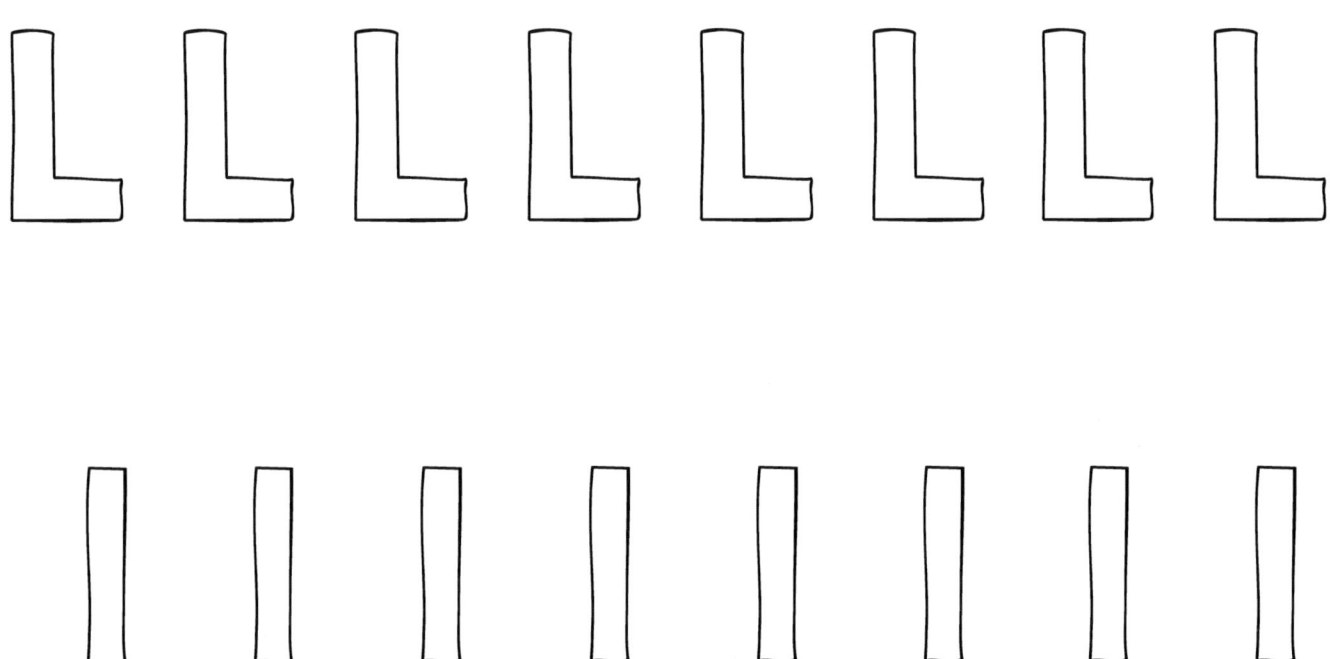

What do we have over there? That is a **M**eerkat.

A Meerkat has small legs and a long tail.

She is known as the "watcher" of the jungle.

She likes to stand and look around everywhere.

She is staring at you now to colour her hair.

Read and colour the letter.

M M M M M M M

m m m m m m

This is a **N**ewt.

A Newt has a long, thin and slimy body.
He has four legs and a long tail like a lizard.
He loves to live in humid, wet grass and ponds.
You can colour his body, what do you say?

Read and colour the letter.

N N N N N N N N

n n n n n n n n

This is an Ostrich.

An Ostrich is the largest bird in the jungle.

He can run very fast but cannot fly.

He has a long neck and a black body with white feathers.

Now you see him, colour his feathers before he runs.

Read and colour the letter.

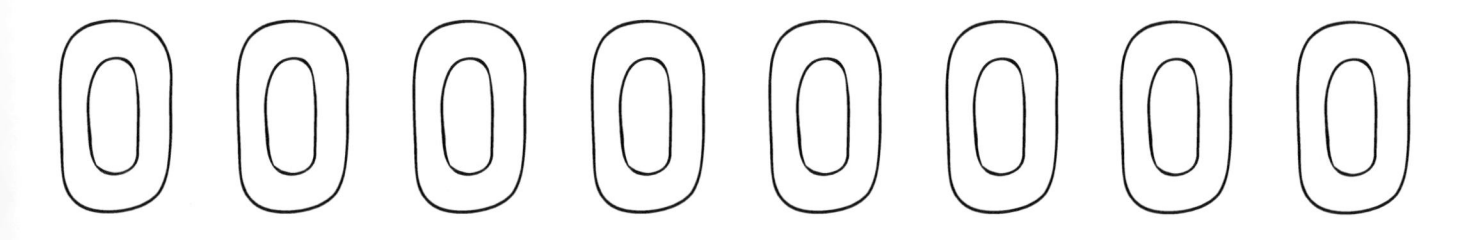

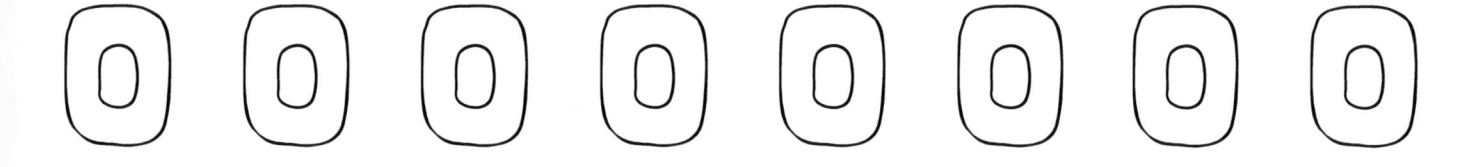

O O O O O O O O

o o o o o o o o

This is a Pangolin.

The Pangolin is a scaly-skinned mammal with tiny legs.

She lives in hollow trees or burrows.

Sometimes she can roll into a ball!

Quick, colour her scaly skin before she rolls into a ball down the hole!

Read and colour the letter.

P P P P P P P P P

p p p p p p p p p

This is a Quail.

A Quail is a small bird with a small tail and tiny beak.

Let's get closer and have a sneaky peek!

Oh, look! His feathers have many different colours.

Let's colour his feathers nice and bright.

Read and colour the letter.

Q Q Q Q Q Q Q Q

q q q q q q q q

This is a Rhinoceros.

A Rhinoceros is a big and heavy jungle animal.

She has a thick grey body, small ears and pointy horns.

She likes to eat grass all day.

Colour her horns before she runs away to eat more grass.

Read and colour the letter.

R R R R R R R R

r r r r r r r r

What do we have here? This is a **S**tork.

A stork is a bird with long beak and long thin legs.

He loves walking in the lake, fishing with his beak.

Oh, no! His legs have disappeared!

Do your magic and make his long thin legs appear again.

Read and colour the letter.

S S S S S S S S

S S S S S S S S

This is a **T**oad.

A Toad has wide eyes and a slimy body.

He lives near the lake and sits on a large green leaf.

He likes to hop from one place to another with a loud croak.

Let's colour his body before he hops!

Read and colour the letter.

T T T T T T T T

t t t t t t t t

This is an Upupa.

An Upupa is a beautiful, colourful bird and has a long beak.

She lives in nests on either trees or burrows.

She has a crown of feathers: yellow and black.

Finish her crown with the colours you have. You know how!

Read and colour the letter.

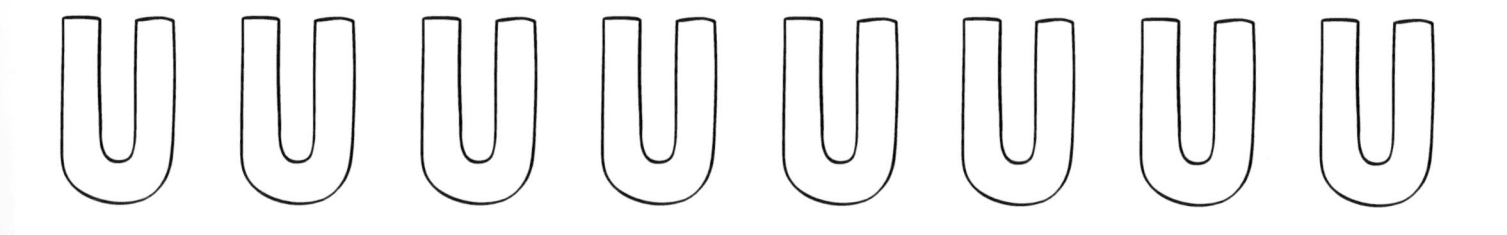

U U U U U U U

u u u u u u u u

This is a Vulture.

A Vulture is a big flying bird.

He has large wings, sharp claws and a sharp beak.

He has black and grey feathers on his body but no feathers on his head.

Instead, his head is bare and grey, let's colour it in.

Read and colour the letter.

V V V V V V V V

V V V V V V V V

This is a Wildebeest.

Wildebeest is always on the move with his family.

He is shy sometimes and likes to eat grass.

He has short horns and a beard from his neck to his belly.

His beard is missing it seems; can you please colour it in?

Read and colour the letter.

W W W W W W W

w w w w w w

This is a Xerus.

A Xerus is known as the African squirrel.

She has a short body with white stripes on the sides.

She lives in burrows and likes to eat nuts, seeds and leaves.

Mummy Xerus would like you to colour her body, please.

Read and colour the letter.

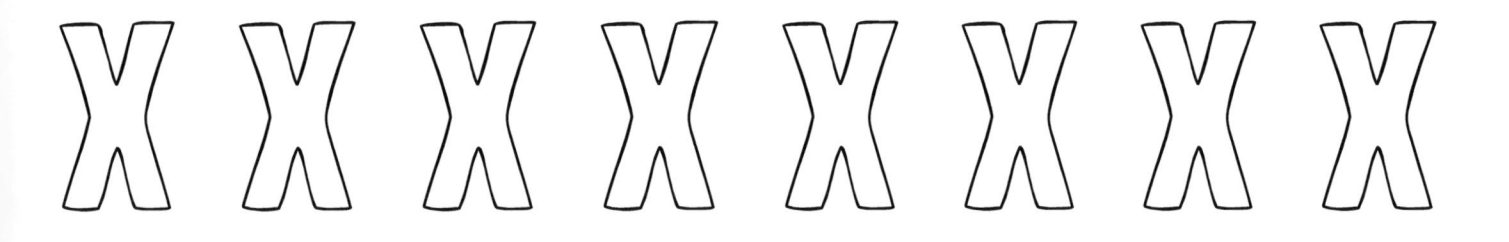

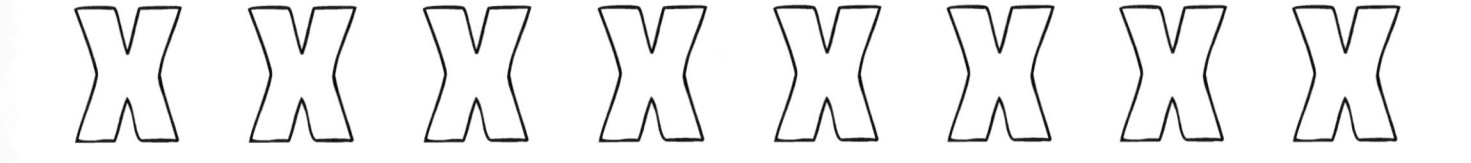

X X X X X X X X

x x x x x x x x

This is a Yellow Mongoose.

Yellow Mongoose is a small animal, sometimes called the Red Meerkat.

She has yellow furry hair, big eyes and small ears.

She also likes to live in burrows with her family. Quick!

Colour her furry body before she runs into her burrow.

Read and colour the letter.

Y Y Y Y Y Y Y Y

y y y y y y y y

Zebo is a **Z**ebra.

Zebra is the African cousin of a horse.

She has black and white stripes over her body, except for her belly.

She is very friendly and like many of her friends, eats grass too.

Some of Zebo's stripes are missing; can you please colour them in?

Read and colour the letter.

Z Z Z Z Z Z Z Z

Z Z Z Z Z Z Z Z

Now you have met some of our friends on the alphabet.

Did you have fun "..Megan..."?

We all had fun as well!

And guess what? We have a special song.

Let's sing it together:

"Eva, Bobo, "..Megan.." and friends are having fun

Holding hands with everyone

Out in the jungle with all our friends

Going around to explore, the fun never ends!"

Join us on our adventures again "..Megan.."

You can find out how special all our friends are in our next book.

Bye and see you soon!

Learn with Eva and Bobo

Comments and Reviews: evabobobooks@gmail.com

Printed in Great Britain
by Amazon

16754057R00038